Go with the Flow

Written and Illustrated
by Holly Wilkin

To Bradley and Daisy.

Enjoy the ride…

Two fluffy bears, in a little wooden boat,
"Let go of the oars" cried Betty, "let's see if we can float!"

Bertie gripped the oars as tightly as can be,
If he let them go, they could drift out to sea!

Bertie didn't like to take risks,
but Betty loved an adventure!
They really were an unlikely pair,
but had a special friendship.

Betty had encouraged Bertie
to come along that day.
Bertie was a compliant bear,
he didn't get much say…

The butterflies danced,
the fish flitted under the clear river…
They were drifting so far from home,
the thought made Bertie shiver.

What if the boat got snapped in two,
or they were taken hostage by pirates?
What if, what if, what if…
the thoughts just wouldn't be quiet!

It was then that Bertie noticed,
that the river had got wide.
He could no longer see the land
as they bobbed along the tide.

Betty giggled gleefully
as they rowed into the great big wave.
But Bertie gripped on tighter -
he wasn't feeling so brave!

Bertie rowed much faster now,
out of the waves and foam,
afraid that if he let go
they might never make it home.

"Look, Bertie! Look…", sang Betty excitedly.

Three beautiful dolphins jumped right out of the sea!

Bertie didn't dare to look,
he just wanted to be in bed.
When snuggled in his fluffy covers,
he didn't feel any dread.

Betty smiled and laid her paws
on Bertie's shaking knee.
"Just let go of the oars", she softly whispered,
"you can always trust in me".

Feeling really tired now,
from holding on so tight,
Bertie slowly dropped the oars
and looked into the night.

"Night?!" exclaimed Bertie,
wondering what his fear had been about.
Suddenly he realised that when you sit and worry,
you really do miss out.

As the little wooden boat
drifted towards the stream,
Bertie suddenly realised
things wasn't as they seemed.

If Bertie hadn't been so worried
he might have enjoyed the day more.
Instead he worried what may go wrong,
not letting go of the oar.

Two fluffy bears sat quietly side by side.
Once Bertie started to relax,
he really enjoyed the ride.

This time he looked and listened,
appreciating the wonderful view.
As all of his fears and worries melted away,
he learnt something new…

Going on a new adventure can be fun,
but scary too.
Sometimes we have to explore the unknown
but that's ok to do.

Bertie was no longer worried
about how this story may end,
instead he took a big deep breath
and smiled right at his friend.

Meet the bears

Betty and Bertie are the first two well-being bears to make an appearance within children's literature. When creating this story, I wanted to use my extensive experience within the educational sector to promote a sense of positive well-being.
Within the well-being series, children are able to gain an understanding of self awareness, and build resilience in appreciating that it's okay to be themselves.

This series was written with the intention of supporting young children to live lives with meaning, especially in understanding where they belong in the world. Bertie, for example, is a worried character but soon develops an appreciation for his adventure with the support and love from his patient friend, Betty. Betty portrays an adventurous little bear, who thrives off of her high satisfaction for life and all of its wonders!

I hope that you love reading the series as much as I enjoyed creating the bears; after all, being you is a pretty wonderful gift.
Live life. Laugh often. Love whole heartedly because life is the greatest adventure of all.

Love Holly

Printed in Great Britain
by Amazon

26862898R00018